Essential (

COMPREHENSIVE, STEP BY STEP COOKING

Italian
Dishes

BUDGET
BOOKS

Food Editor: Neil Hargreaves
Cover Design: Budget Books
Prepress: Graphic Print Group

 Essential Cooking Series: Italian Dishes
First published in 2008 by Budget Books Pty Ltd
45–55 Fairchild Street
Heatherton, Victoria, 3202, Australia

10 9 8 7 6
13   12 11 10 09

Disclaimer: The nutritional information listed under each recipe does not
include the nutrient content of garnishes or any accompaniments not listed
in specific quantitites in the ingredient list. The nutritional information for
each recipe is an estimate only, and may vary depending on the brand of
ingredients used, and due to natural biological variations in the composition
of natural foods such as meat, fish, fruit and vegetables. The nutritional
information was calculated by using Foodworks dietary analysis software
(Version 3, Xyris Software Pty Ltd, Highgate Hill, Queensland, Australia) based
on the Australian food composition tables and food manufacturers' data.
Where not specified, ingredients are always analysed as average or medium,
not small or large.

ISBN: 978 1 7418 1463 7

Printed and bound in China

Contents

An introduction to Italian dishes

Italian cooking, in the minds of some people, is synonymous with pasta. It's true that pasta is very popular in Italy, but so too is rice, which grows in northern Italy. Soups are also very popular, varying from region to region and from season to season. Meats, fish, crustaceans and shellfish with vegetables (either cooked or served as salads) make up the secondo piatto (second course). Fresh fruit and a variety of cheeses complete the meal, which is then finished with a cup of espresso coffee.

EATING HABITS

Traditionally, the main meal in Italy is lunch. With most offices, shops and schools closed between 1pm and 4pm, and with some public offices closing down for the day at 2pm, lunch in an Italian household is on the table any time after 1pm. For those who have only a one-hour break, lunch is still a very important meal. Whether at home, in the restaurant around the corner from the office, or at the mensa (the refectory or canteen), lunch is comprised of the primo piatto (first course) of soup, rice or pasta, followed by the secondo piatto (second course) of meat or fish, together with cheeses, vegetables or salad, and finally fruit.

The evening meal, any time after 8pm, could be a lighter version of lunch. However, the pasta is often replaced by a light soup with very small pasta-shapes cooked for only a few minutes, and a frittata might replace the meat dish. For the evening meal, the emphasis is on easily digestible foods: vegetables, salads, cheeses and fruit. Bread (but not butter) is part of every meal. Italians prefer to have a very light breakfast: a cappuccino or an espresso coffee, and perhaps a small cake from the local coffee-bar on the way to work. Caffè latte and biscuits, a thick slice of homemade cake or bread and butter with jam make up the more homely Italian breakfast.

THE DAILY BREAD

Bread has an almost transcendental role in Italian eating habits, and bakers are the high priests of Italian cooking. During the 1950s and 1960s there were attempts to replace the local panetteria (bread shop) with mass-produced bread, but common sense, and the Italian love for traditional bread-making, defeated the invading industrial moguls. The panettieri (bakers) resumed their traditional role in the lives of Italians. Today, thousands of panettieri prepare regional breads, differing in shape, taste, texture

and ingredients, and continue the tradition that started soon after 168 BC, when freed Macedonian slaves baked bread for the Roman Empire.

The popular pasta dura bread, typical of Emilia-Romagna, is considered to be the oldest type of bread, going back to Egypt via Rome. The most extraordinary breads come from the two largest Italian islands – Sicily and Sardinia. Sicilian bread, with its unusual shapes and sprinkling of sesame seeds, bears the marks of the Saracen occupation, but perhaps the most unusual bread is the carta da musica (music paperbread) from Sardinia. Made from unleavened dough, this wafer-thin bread was originally used by Sardinian shepherds during their lengthy periods away from home. Today, however, the carta da musica (so-called because, when eaten, it sounds like music) has become a symbol of refined living and discerning cuisine.

STEPPING BACK IN TIME

The history of Italian gastronomy goes back to pre-Roman times, and consists of a long list of 'imported' and 'exported' foods. The first Romans were shepherds and farmers who soon learned how to evaporate sea water to produce salt for their sheep. When the production of salt was surplus to their needs, they started to export to Greek settlements in the south and to the Etruscans in the north. It was the beginning of a very profitable trade, as testified by the name of one of the main roads leading to Rome – the Via Salaria (Salt Road) – which was used by Roman salt exporters.

By the second century BC, Roman cuisine had become more complex. Herbs and spices brought back to Rome by Roman legionnaires were added to basic foods, and different sauces were developed – including the garum sauce (a fish-based sauce) and the agrodolce sauce, still in use today. These sauces were indiscriminately splashed on every dish.

The extravagant and excessive cooking and eating habits of the new-rich in the last days of the Roman Empire are depicted in the film *Satyricon*. Not until the banquets of the Renaissance was there again such incredible gastronomical extravagance.

The Crusaders introduced buckwheat to Italy, and then to Europe. They also reintroduced lemons and spices, many of which had been known to the Romans. Marco Polo did not introduce noodles to Italy, but his trip to the East eventually led to the opening up of a direct route to the spices of the Far East, and his countrymen, the Venetians, became wealthy importers and exporters of spices and coffee. With the discovery of the New World, peppers, tomatoes and potatoes (among other palatable foods) were introduced to Italy and soon became part of Italian culinary traditions. Maize, which is now used to make polenta, was accepted by Italian palates in 1650. By the end of the 17th century, Italian cooking and eating habits had reached full maturity.

Italian regional foods have migrated from their places of origin. Such was the destiny of the Neapolitan pizza, which at first crawled rather slowly to other parts of Italy, and then expanded throughout the world and is now known virtually everywhere now.

A CULINARY HISTORY

It took centuries to perfect the cooking habits and techniques that we now recognise as 'Italian cooking'; centuries to move from the plain, the bland and the basic to the extravagant, the astonishing and the complex. Roman soldiers and citizens of the second century BC ate a basic polenta-type dish, but by the time of the declining Roman Empire there were the extraordinary banquets of the rich and famous.

With the fall of the Roman Empire, hordes of barbarians invaded the peninsula, and cooking became plain once more, with very few herbs to enhance flavours. During the Renaissance, culinary excesses were counterbalanced by the less flamboyant meals of the wealthy Florentine merchants, and the less-rich Florentines, who had an even simpler form of cooking. In fact, apart from festivities or celebrations, the Florentines of the Renaissance generally preferred a rather uncomplicated style of cooking. In so doing they were following the advice of Platina, librarian of the Vatican. In his book *De Honesta Voluptate ac Valetudine (Concerning Honest Pleasure and Well-Being)*, Platina recommended moderation. The success of Platina's book clearly indicates the importance of the art of cooking during the 15th century.

The increasing interest in gastronomy is further illustrated by the foundation of the first modern cooking academy, the Compagnia del Paiolo (Company of the Cauldron) in Florence in the late 15th century. One of its most famous members was the painter Andrea del Sarto who prepared for the Compagnia a dish representing a temple resting on a multi-coloured gelatine. Sausages and wedges of Parmesan cheese were used to represent the temple's columns. Inside the temple was a music-stand holding a book, with pages made of sheets of pasta, and the musical notes represented by grains of pepper.

It is this sort of extravagant combination of ingredients (and richness of colours) that we find again, four centuries later, in Marinetti's *Futurist Cookbook*. It is interesting to see that cooking utensils penetrated one of the most formal institutions of the 16th century: the Accademia della Crusca (Academy of the Bran). Founded in 1582, the academy was founded in order to establish and safeguard the correct use of the Tuscan language. One of the symbols used by the academy was, and still is, the wooden shovel used by bakers. It represents the 'sifting' of the good usage of the language from the bad!

Florence was the cradle of the Renaissance in every field, including gastronomy, and the influence of Florence on the rest of the then-known world was unchallenged. But it was not the uncomplicated and healthy cooking habits recommended by Platina that conquered French palates. It was the rich, voluptuous and sumptuous cuisine of the Florentine court that appealed to Francis I, and which his daughter-in-law (Catherine de' Medici) took back to France. A new gastronomic era was beginning for the French Court, and new horizons were opening up – with all the subtleties and variations of Italian cuisine.

Today, Italian cuisine remains one of the most popular styles of cooking around the world.

Asparagus with pecorino and pancetta

INGREDIENTS

500 g asparagus
juice of 1 lemon
100 ml extra virgin olive oil
sea salt
freshly ground black pepper
8 thin slices of pancetta, cut into
  pieces
pecorino cheese, shaved

serves 4

PREPARATION TIME
4 minutes

COOKING TIME
4 minutes

1 Trim off the thick asparagus ends and cook asparagus in boiling
water for 4 minutes until tender but still crisp. Run under cold
water until asparagus is cool, then dry with paper towel.

2 For the dressing, place the lemon juice in a bowl and slowly add
the oil, whisking, until thick. Season with salt and pepper.

3 Pour the dressing over asparagus, and serve with the pancetta
and pecorino cheese shavings.

NUTRITIONAL VALUE PER SERVE   FAT 22 G   CARBOHYDRATE 1.5 G   PROTEIN 7 G

Black olive fontina pâté

INGREDIENTS

8 cloves garlic
220 g fontina cheese, cut into
  small cubes
1 cup oil-cured black olives, pitted
¼ cup olive oil
1 loaf of crusty bread to serve
serves 4

PREPARATION TIME
5 minutes, plus
30 minutes refrigeration

COOKING TIME
30 minutes

1 Preheat the oven to 180°C. Wrap the garlic cloves in foil and bake
for 30 minutes. Remove from oven, open foil and let cool slightly.

2 While the garlic cloves are cooling, melt the fontina cheese in a
double-boiler over simmering water, stirring until smooth.

3 Using a food processor, blend olives, garlic and olive oil for
20 seconds. Add melted cheese and pulse for 10 more seconds
until combined.

4 Spoon out into a serving dish and cover tightly with the plastic
wrap, leaving no room for air at the top. Refrigerate for 30 minutes
before serving. Serve with crusty bread.

NUTRITIONAL VALUE PER SERVE   FAT 18.5 G   CARBOHYDRATE 6 G   PROTEIN 10 G

Bruschetta with bocconcini and basil

INGREDIENTS

1 ciabatta loaf
$\frac{1}{4}$ cup olive oil
$\frac{1}{3}$ cup sun-dried tomato paste
180 g bocconcini cheese, each ball
   sliced into 5
$\frac{1}{2}$ cup basil leaves, shredded or whole
serves 4

PREPARATION TIME
4 minutes

COOKING TIME
3 minutes

1 Slice the bread into 2 cm thick slices.

2 Grill ciabatta slices on each side for 2–3 minutes.

3 Brush ciabatta with olive oil, spread with sun-dried tomato paste, and top with bocconcini slices and basil.

NUTRITIONAL VALUE PER SERVE   FAT 21.5 G   CARBOHYDRATE 34 G   PROTEIN 13 G

Mozzarella with garlic and caper berries

INGREDIENTS

500 g fresh mozzarella cheese
dressing
2 cloves garlic, chopped
4 tablespoons olive oil
2 tablespoons balsamic vinegar
1 tablespoon fresh oregano, chopped
1 teaspoon salt
½ teaspoon ground black pepper
garnish
caper berries
black olives
fresh oregano
serves 4

PREPARATION TIME
10 minutes

1 Slice the mozzarella into 1 cm slices. Place slices on to a serving dish.

2 Place the dressing ingredients in a bowl and stir to combine. Pour the dressing over the sliced mozzarella.

3 Garnish with the caper berries, olives and oregano.

NUTRITIONAL VALUE PER SERVE   FAT 18.5 G   CARBOHYDRATE 3.5 G   PROTEIN 0.5 G

Roasted garlic polenta

INGREDIENTS

2 bulbs garlic
1 shallot, finely diced
1 teaspoon salt
1$^1/_2$ L water
250 g fast cooking polenta
50 g butter
50 g parmesan cheese, grated
$^1/_4$ bunch basil, chopped

serves 4

1 Preheat the oven to 200°C. Wrap the garlic in foil and roast for 45 minutes to 1 hour. Remove from the oven and squeeze out the garlic from the skins.

2 Place the shallot, salt and water into a saucepan and bring to the boil. Pour the polenta into the boiling water and stir continuously for 5 minutes.

3 Stir the garlic through the polenta. Stir through butter and parmesan. Cook for 2 minutes. Serve topped with basil accompanied by chargrilled vegetables.

PREPARATION TIME
3 minutes

COOKING TIME
52 minutes

| NUTRITIONAL VALUE PER SERVE | FAT 10.5 G | CARBOHYDRATE 29 G | PROTEIN 7 G |

Focaccia bread

INGREDIENTS

50 g dried yeast

1 teaspoon honey

¼ cup warm water

750 g plain flour

¼ cup extra virgin olive oil,
plus 1 tablespoon for
brushing over the focaccia

½ cup black olives, pitted

handful sea salt

2 sprigs rosemary, pulled off
the stalks

serves 4

1 Dissolve the yeast and honey in the warm water. Place the flour onto work surface and make a well in the centre. Pour the yeast mixture and the olive oil into the well. Work the flour into the wet mixture slowly; add more warm water if necessary.

2 Once the mixture has formed into a dough, knead for around 10 minutes, until the dough is smooth and elastic. Place into a large oiled bowl and cover with a damp cloth. Let the dough rise for 2 hours.

3 Preheat the oven to 200°C.

4 Grease a large baking tray. Remove the risen dough from the bowl and punch out the dough, then place on the tray and roll out the dough to the size of the tray. Brush with the remaining olive oil. Scatter the olives over the dough and press them into the dough. Sprinkle a good handful of sea salt over the dough and lastly the rosemary. Place into the oven and bake for 15–20 minutes or until golden brown. Remove and cool before cutting.

PREPARATION TIME
2 hours 15 minutes

COOKING TIME
20 minutes

NUTRITIONAL VALUE PER SERVE	FAT 17 G	CARBOHYDRATE 94 G	PROTEIN 13.5 G

Aioli italia

INGREDIENTS

3 cloves garlic
salt
1 egg yolk, at room temperature
juice of half a lemon
1 cup light olive oil
white pepper
makes around 1¼ cups

PREPARATION TIME
3 minutes

1 Place garlic and 1 teaspoon salt in a food processor, pulse briefly. Add the egg yolk and lemon juice, and pulse on and off until blended.

2 Slowly add the oil in a steady stream. Add a pinch of white pepper and adjust the salt to taste.

3 To thin out the aioli at any stage, add a small dash of room temperature water and continue adding the remainder of the oil. Use as an accompaniment to vegetables, fish and meats.

NUTRITIONAL VALUE PER SERVE   FAT 39 G   CARBOHYDRATE 0.5 G   PROTEIN 0.5 G

Herbed olive oil sabayon

INGREDIENTS

4 leaves chervil
4 leaves tarragon
4 leaves parsley
2 cups dry white wine
$^1/_2$ cup white-wine vinegar
2 medium shallots, peeled and
  chopped
4 egg yolks
$^2/_3$ cup extra virgin olive oil
salt and freshly ground pepper
makes around 1½ cups

PREPARATION TIME
4 minutes

COOKING TIME
2 minutes

1 Pick the stems off all of the herbs. Heat a heavy-based saucepan and simmer the wine, vinegar, shallots and herb stems together over medium heat to reduce by approximately $^1/_3$ cup in volume. Strain into a pouring jug and keep warm.

2 Put the egg yolks in a blender and then, with the blender running, slowly pour in the warm liquid followed by the olive oil. Turn blender off.

3 Chop and add the herb leaves and salt and pepper to taste, pulse the blender once or twice, then remove to a warm bowl. Serve warm within 1 hour as an accompaniment to vegetables, fish and meats.

NUTRITIONAL VALUE PER SERVE	FAT 14 G	CARBOHYDRATE 0 G	PROTEIN 1 G

Roasted tomato, red capsicum and bread soup

INGREDIENTS

1 kg roma tomatoes
2 red capsicums, roughly chopped
2 tablespoons olive oil
3 cloves garlic, crushed
2 onions, finely chopped
2 teaspoons cumin
1 teaspoon ground coriander
1 L chicken stock
2 slices white bread, crusts removed
  and torn into pieces
1 tablespoon balsamic vinegar
salt and freshly ground pepper to
  taste
parmesan cheese, grated
serves 4

PREPARATION TIME
10 minutes

COOKING TIME
1 hour

1 Preheat the oven to 220°C and cut tomatoes in half.

2 Place tomatoes and capsicums in a lightly oiled baking dish and bake for 20 minutes, or until the skins have blistered. Set aside to cool, then remove skins and roughly chop.

3 Heat the oil in a saucepan, add the garlic and the onion, and cook for 5 minutes or until soft. Add cumin and coriander and cook for 1 minute. Add tomatoes, capsicums and stock to the saucepan, bring to the boil, and simmer for 30 minutes. Add bread, balsamic vinegar, salt and pepper, and cook a further 5–10 minutes.

4 Serve with parmesan cheese, if desired.

NUTRITIONAL VALUE PER SERVE   FAT 13 G   CARBOHYDRATE 17 G   PROTEIN 10.5 G

Jerusalem artichoke soup

INGREDIENTS

50 g butter
6 slices pancetta
1 large onion, peeled and thinly sliced
1 leek, thinly sliced then soaked and
  washed
1 stalk celery, peeled and thinly sliced
2 cloves garlic, peeled
bouquet garni
1 kg jerusalem artichokes, cleaned
  and cut into thick slices
1 small potato, peeled and diced
2 L unsalted chicken stock
salt and freshly ground white pepper
$^3/_4$ cup extra virgin olive oil
serves 4

PREPARATION TIME
35 minutes

COOKING TIME
1 hour 10 minutes

1 Melt the butter in a large saucepan over medium heat. Add the
pancetta and cook for 5 minutes, stirring occasionally. Add the
onion, leek, celery, garlic and the bouquet garni, cook for 5 minutes,
stirring occasionally. Add the artichokes and the potato and cook
for 15 to 20 minutes, stirring occasionally.

2 Add the stock and bring the mixture to the boil. Lower the heat
to a simmer and cook, uncovered, for 35 minutes. Discard the
bouquet garni.

3 Working in batches, purée the soup in a food processor and add
the salt and pepper to taste. Add the olive oil to the soup and bring
to the simmer.

NUTRITIONAL VALUE PER SERVE   FAT 12 G   CARBOHYDRATE 4 G   PROTEIN 3.5 G

Garlic and bean soup

INGREDIENTS

200 g pancetta
8 cloves garlic
1 tablespoon butter
1 onion, finely diced
2 stalks celery, diced
2 L chicken stock
3 roma tomatoes, peeled, seeded
   and diced
2 zucchinis, diced
2 tablespoons fresh thyme
2 bay leaves
425 g can cannellini beans
425 g can borlotti beans
salt and freshly ground black pepper
serves 4

1 Dice the pancetta. Slice the garlic.

2 Melt butter in a large saucepan. Add the onion and garlic and cook until transparent. Add the pancetta and cook for 3 minutes. Add the celery and cook for a further 2 minutes. Add the stock, tomatoes, zucchinis, thyme and bay leaves. Cook for 15 minutes.

3 Add the beans and cook for a further 20 minutes. Season the soup with salt and freshly ground black pepper. Serve in bowls.

PREPARATION TIME
15 minutes

COOKING TIME
40 minutes

NUTRITIONAL VALUE PER SERVE	FAT 14.5 G	CARBOHYDRATE 53 G	PROTEIN 36 G

Spaghetti with garlic and anchovies

INGREDIENTS

500 g spaghetti
6 cloves garlic
pinch of salt
4 tablespoons olive oil, plus extra to serve
1 tablespoon butter
8 anchovies, roughly chopped
½ small bunch of flat-leaf parsley, finely chopped
freshly ground pepper
parmesan cheese, shaved
serves 4

1 Cook spaghetti according to packet directions.

2 Meanwhile, peel the garlic, add a pinch of salt and crush with the flat of a knife to make a fine paste. Heat olive oil and butter in a pan. Add the garlic to the pan and cook for 1 minute. Add the anchovies and cook until they melt into the garlic: approximately 2 minutes.

3 Add the spaghetti and parsley to the garlic and anchovy mix and toss to combine. Season with pepper to taste.

4 Top with shaved parmesan and a drizzle of olive oil.

PREPARATION TIME
8 minutes

COOKING TIME
10 minutes

NUTRITIONAL VALUE PER SERVE	FAT 24.5 G	CARBOHYDRATE 86 G	PROTEIN 16.5 G

Smoked salmon ravioli with lemon dill sauce

INGREDIENTS

125 g smoked salmon pieces
4 egg whites
1½ tablespoons cream
2 teaspoons fresh dill, roughly
  chopped
2–3 tablespoons cornflour
32 wonton skins
1 teaspoon oil
lemon dill sauce
1 tablespoon butter
1 tablespoon flour
¾ cup white wine
¾ cup thickened cream
juice of half a lemon
2 tablespoons dill, roughly chopped
salt and freshly ground black pepper
serves 4

1 Place the salmon, 1 tablespoon of egg white, cream and dill in a food processor, and process until well combined, like a mousse.

2 Sprinkle the cornflour on a work surface and lay wonton skins in rows of four.

3 Brush every second skin around the edge with egg white. On alternate skins, place a teaspoon of mixture in the middle. Place the other skins on top and gently pinch around the mixture, so they look like pillows or rounds.

4 Half fill a large saucepan with water, add 1 teaspoon of oil, bring to the boil and add 2–3 cups ravioli. Cook for 2–3 minutes. Set aside and cover with plastic wrap.

5 To make the lemon dill sauce, melt the butter in a saucepan, add the flour and cook for 1 minute. Add the wine and stir until smooth, then add the cream and lemon juice. Bring to the boil and reduce until sauce has a pouring consistency.

6 To serve, add the dill, salt and pepper to the sauce and pour over the ravioli.

PREPARATION TIME
20 minutes

COOKING TIME
15 minutes

NUTRITIONAL VALUE PER SERVE	FAT 30 G	CARBOHYDRATE 13 G	PROTEIN 10 G

Pæsani pasta with rocket and spicy pancetta

INGREDIENTS

500 g fusilli pæsani
1 tablespoon extra virgin olive oil
2 cloves garlic, crushed
100g hot pancetta, roughly chopped
1 cup tomato pasta sauce
100 g semi-sun-dried tomatoes
1 bunch rocket, washed and drained
salt and freshly ground black pepper
parmesan cheese, shaved
serves 4

PREPARATION TIME
3 minutes

COOKING TIME
15 minutes

1 Cook pasta in boiling salted water until al dente. Drain and set aside.

2 Heat oil in a saucepan, add garlic and pancetta and cook for 2 minutes or until garlic is soft and flavours are well combined.

3 Add the pasta, tomato sauce, semi-sun-dried tomatoes, rocket, salt and pepper to the pan, and heat through.

4 Serve with parmesan cheese.

NUTRITIONAL VALUE PER SERVE	FAT 13 G	CARBOHYDRATE 101 G	PROTEIN 25.5 G

Linguine with prawns, zucchini flowers and olive oil sauce

INGREDIENTS
800 g linguine
12 zucchini flowers
3 cloves garlic, crushed
1/2 cup extra virgin olive oil
1 large onion, diced
12 prawns, shells and heads removed
1 tablespoon thyme, chopped
juice of 1 lemon
salt and freshly ground black pepper
serves 4

PREPARATION TIME
12 minutes

COOKING TIME
10 minutes

1 Boil water for pasta in a saucepan and add the linguine.

2 Cut the flowers off the zucchini. Slice the baby zucchini into rounds and coat with the crushed garlic and some of the olive oil.

3 Slice zucchini flowers into quarters.

4 Sweat the onion in the remaining olive oil, add prawns and zucchini and fry slowly until just cooked.

5 When pasta is al dente, drain and combine with the thyme, zucchini flowers, lemon juice and season with salt and pepper.

| NUTRITIONAL VALUE PER SERVE | FAT 31.5 G | CARBOHYDRATE 157 G | PROTEIN 38 G |

Butterflied quail with lemon and sage leaves

INGREDIENTS

2 tablespoons olive oil
1 tablespoon lemon juice
$\frac{1}{2}$ teaspoon lemon zest
1 clove garlic, crushed
freshly ground pepper
sea salt
1 tablespoon olive oil, extra
4 quails, butterflied
1 bunch sage leaves: 1 tablespoon
  chopped, the rest for garnish
$\frac{1}{4}$ cup chicken stock
serves 4

PREPARATION TIME
10 minutes

COOKING TIME
30 minutes

1 Preheat the oven to 180°C.

2 Combine the olive oil, lemon juice, lemon zest, garlic, pepper and salt in a bowl. Set aside.

3 Heat the extra oil in a large frying pan, add the quail and the chopped sage leaves, and brown quickly. Set aside.

4 To the pan, add the lemon juice mixture and the chicken stock. Return to the heat, bring to the boil and simmer for 1 minute to reduce, stirring with a wooden spoon.

5 Pour the sauce over the quail, transfer to an ovenproof dish and bake in the oven for 20–25 minutes. Garnish with whole sage leaves.

NUTRITIONAL VALUE PER SERVE   FAT 21 G   CARBOHYDRATE 0.5 G   PROTEIN 21 G

Chicken with basil cream sauce

INGREDIENTS

3 tablespoons flour
salt and freshly ground black pepper
4 chicken breasts
1 tablespoon olive oil
1 tablespoon butter
basil cream sauce
1 tablespoon butter
2 cloves garlic, crushed
$^1/_2$ cup chicken stock
$^1/_2$ cup cream
$^1/_4$ cup lemon juice
2 tablespoons basil, finely chopped
freshly ground pepper
sea salt
serves 4

PREPARATION TIME
5 minutes

COOKING TIME
15 minutes

1 Combine the flour, pepper and salt in a bowl and coat the chicken evenly with the mixture, shaking off the excess.

2 Heat the oil and butter in a pan, add the chicken and cook over medium heat for 5–6 minutes each side. Remove from the pan and keep warm.

3 To make the basil cream sauce, wipe out the pan, heat the butter, add the garlic and cook for 2 minutes. Add the chicken stock, cream and lemon juice, bring to the boil and reduce a little.

4 Just before serving, add the basil, season with pepper and salt and pour the sauce over the chicken.

NUTRITIONAL VALUE PER SERVE	FAT 42 G	CARBOHYDRATE 8 G	PROTEIN 63.5 G

Chicken saltimbocca

INGREDIENTS

4 small chicken breasts
2–3 tablespoons butter
220 g mozzarella, sliced into
  8 rounds
8 slices prosciutto
12 sage leaves
sauce
2 teaspoons sage, roughly chopped
½ cup white wine
¼ cup chicken stock

serves 4

1 Using a meat mallet, pound the chicken until thin.

2 Heat the butter in a pan, add the chicken and brown quickly on both sides. Remove from the pan and top each breast with 2 slices mozzarella, 2 slices prosciutto and 2–3 sage leaves. Secure with toothpicks.

3 Under a hot grill, cook chicken for approximately 2 minutes, until cheese has just started to melt. Set aside.

4 To make the sauce, reheat the butter, add the sage and cook for 1 minute. Add the white wine and stock and reduce the sauce slightly.

5 Pour the sauce over the chicken, and serve immediately.

PREPARATION TIME
12 minutes

COOKING TIME
6 minutes

| NUTRITIONAL VALUE PER SERVE | FAT 34 G | CARBOHYDRATE 0.5 G | PROTEIN 59 G |

Garlic and lemon mussels

INGREDIENTS

2 tablespoons olive oil
1 kg mussels
6 cloves garlic, finely chopped
1 chilli, sliced
$^1/_2$ bunch basil leaves, roughly
  chopped
4 roma tomatoes, diced
1 cup white wine
1 teaspoon salt
freshly ground black pepper
1 lemon, cut into wedges
serves 4

1 Heat the oil in a heavy-based saucepan until almost smoking. Add the mussels. They should make a popping sound when they hit the oil. Cook for 1 minute.

2 Add the garlic, chilli, basil, tomatoes and white wine. Cover with a lid and cook for a further 4 minutes.

3 Discard any mussels that do not open during cooking. Season with salt and pepper. Serve with lemon wedges.

PREPARATION TIME
10 minutes

COOKING TIME
5 minutes

NUTRITIONAL VALUE PER SERVE   FAT **14** G   CARBOHYDRATE **16** G   PROTEIN **13.5** G

Salmon cutlets with dill hollandaise sauce

INGREDIENTS

2 tablespoons extra virgin olive oil,
    plus extra for grilling
1 tablespoon lemon juice
$^2/_3$ teaspoon coarse black pepper
4 salmon cutlets, each 220–250 g
1 bunch asparagus
dill hollandaise sauce
85 ml white-wine vinegar
freshly ground black pepper
$^1/_4$ cup water
4 egg yolks
220 g unsalted butter, melted
2 tablespoons lemon juice
3 tablespoons fresh dill, chopped
salt and freshly ground black pepper
serves 4

PREPARATION TIME
10 minutes, plus
3 hours marinating

COOKING TIME
20 minutes

1 Combine oil, lemon juice and pepper in a large ceramic dish. Add salmon cutlets and leave to marinate for 3 hours.

2 To make the sauce, put vinegar, pepper and water in a small saucepan. Bring to the boil, then reduce until 1 tablespoon of the liquid is left.

3 Place egg yolks and vinegar mixture in a food processor and process for 1 minute. With the processor still running, gradually add the hot melted butter and blend until thick.

4 Add lemon juice, dill and salt and pepper to taste, and keep warm.

5 Heat a lightly oiled chargrill pan, or preheat a grill. Cook salmon cutlets for 2–3 minutes each side, or until done to your liking. Trim the asparagus and blanch it in a bowl of boiling water for 2–3 minutes.

6 Serve fish with hollandaise sauce and asparagus on the side.

NUTRITIONAL VALUE PER SERVE	FAT 80.5 G	CARBOHYDRATE 1.5 G	PROTEIN 47 G

Calamari in garlic and capers

INGREDIENTS

4 calamari tubes
poaching liquid
1 small carrot, peeled and chopped
1 small onion, peeled and chopped
$\frac{1}{2}$ bunch thyme
8 cloves garlic
750 ml water
juice and zest of 1 lemon
500 g capers
marinade
1 teaspoon cumin
100 ml extra virgin olive oil
juice of 1 lemon
$\frac{1}{2}$ teaspoon salt
$\frac{1}{2}$ teaspoon ground black pepper
8 sprigs lemon thyme
salad
2 small heads radicchio
1 witlof
2 teaspoons capers
$\frac{1}{2}$ cup flat-leaf parsley, chopped
serves 4

1 Place all the ingredients for the poaching liquid in a saucepan, bring to the boil and simmer for 10 minutes.

2 Meanwhile, clean the calamari tubes under running water. Place into the simmering poaching liquid for around 2 minutes. Remove the garlic cloves from the poaching liquid and slice. Remove the calamari from the poaching liquid and cut into 5 cm wide strips.

3 Place the ingredients for the marinade in a bowl, add the sliced garlic and mix together. Add the sliced calamari to the marinade and refrigerate for 30 minutes.

4 Wash the radicchio and witlof and discard the outer leaves. Place in a bowl with the capers and chopped parsley. Remove the calamari from the marinade, add it to the salad and use $\frac{1}{2}$ cup of the marinade as a dressing.

PREPARATION TIME
20 minutes, plus 30 minutes refrigeration

COOKING TIME
12 minutes

NUTRITIONAL VALUE PER SERVE   FAT 32 G   CARBOHYDRATE 1.5 G   PROTEIN 17 G

Blue-eyed cod with aioli and parmesan potatoes

INGREDIENTS

1 clove garlic, chopped
2 tablespoons olive oil
1 tablespoon lemon juice
4 blue-eyed cod cutlets
1 quantity aioli (see recipe page 18)
handful of basil leaves
parmesan potatoes
400 g potatoes, peeled and cubed
1 tablespoon olive oil
1 tablespoon butter
1 tablespoon parmesan cheese,
   grated
serves 4

PREPARATION TIME
10 minutes, plus
1 hour marinating

COOKING TIME
26 minutes

1 Combine the garlic, olive oil and lemon juice in a dish, and marinate the fish cutlets for 1 hour.

2 Grease a grill or frying pan and cook fish for 3 minutes on each side.

3 To make the parmesan potatoes, place them in a saucepan with salted water and boil until potatoes are almost cooked, but still a little hard in the centre. Drain.

4 Heat the oil and butter in a pan, add the potatoes and cook until brown. Add the cheese and cook until potatoes are crisp.

5 Add basil leaves to the aioli when adding the garlic and serve the fish with the aioli (see recipe on page 18) and parmesan potatoes.

NUTRITIONAL VALUE PER SERVE   FAT **19.5** G   CARBOHYDRATE **14** G   PROTEIN **31** G

Passionfruit zabaglione with fresh berries

INGREDIENTS

5 egg yolks
½ cup caster sugar
½ cup sweet white wine
85 ml passionfruit pulp
125 g blueberries
150 g raspberries
150 g strawberries
serves 4–6

PREPARATION TIME
10 minutes

COOKING TIME
15 minutes

1 Combine egg yolks and sugar in a heatproof bowl and beat
until thick and pale. Beat through the sweet wine, and place the
bowl over a saucepan of simmering water. Continue to beat for
15 minutes or until the mixture is very thick, not allowing the
bowl to heat too much. The mixture is ready when it forms soft
mounds.

2 Remove the bowl from the heat and continue beating for a
further 5 minutes, or until the mixture has cooled. Fold through
the passionfruit pulp and serve with the fresh berries.

NUTRITIONAL VALUE PER SERVE   FAT 5 G   CARBOHYDRATE 28 G   PROTEIN 4 G

Frangelico chocolate cake

INGREDIENTS

100 g dark chocolate, chopped
50 g butter
3 eggs, separated
¼ cup caster sugar
2 tablespoons self-raising flour,
 sifted
¼ cup ground hazelnuts
25 ml frangelico liqueur
sauce
180 g raspberries
2 tablespoons icing sugar
1 tablespoon lemon juice
serves 4

1 Preheat the oven to 190°C. Melt the chocolate and butter over hot water, remove from the heat and stir in egg yolks, caster sugar, flour, hazelnuts and frangelico.

2 Beat the egg whites until soft peaks form. Fold lightly into the chocolate mixture and pour into a greased and lined 12 cm round baking tin and bake for 35–40 minutes, or until cake shrinks slightly from sides of tin.

3 To make the raspberry sauce, place raspberries, icing sugar and lemon juice in a food processor and blend until smooth. Strain, and add a little water if the mixture is too thick.

4 Serve cake cut into wedges, with raspberry sauce and cream.

PREPARATION TIME
15 minutes

COOKING TIME
45 minutes

NUTRITIONAL VALUE PER SERVE	FAT 25 G	CARBOHYDRATE 40 G	PROTEIN 7.5 G

Lemon and olive oil semifreddo

INGREDIENTS

6 egg yolks
³/₄ cup sugar
¹/₂ cup olive oil
3 cups milk
1 cup double cream
juice of 1 lemon
40 ml limoncello liqueur
figs and honey to serve
serves 4

1 Beat the egg yolks and sugar until light in colour and thick in consistency. Slowly blend in olive oil until combined.

2 Combine the milk and cream in a large heavy-based saucepan. Bring to a medium heat, until the mixture starts to simmer. Add a cup of the hot milk to the eggs, whisking thoroughly, and repeat with remaining milk.

3 Return the mixture to the saucepan and stir quickly over heat for 3 minutes. When the custard starts to thicken, remove from the heat and strain through a fine mesh strainer. Add the lemon juice and the limoncello. Cool to room temperature. Pour into a tray and freeze until solid.

4 Leave out of freezer for 10 minutes, slice into pieces and serve with fresh figs and honey.

PREPARATION TIME
5 minutes, plus
3 hours refrigeration

COOKING TIME
5 minutes

NUTRITIONAL VALUE PER SERVE	FAT 30 G	CARBOHYDRATE 22 G	PROTEIN 4.5 G

Lemon crema crunch

INGREDIENTS

6 egg yolks (room temperature)
1 whole egg (room temperature)
600 ml double cream
3 drops vanilla extract
1 sprig rosemary
$^1/_2$ cup caster sugar
zest of 3 lemons
$^1/_2$ cup extra virgin olive oil
iced water
caster sugar, extra
serves 4

PREPARATION TIME
10 minutes

COOKING TIME
50 minutes

1 Preheat the oven to 160°C. Remove eggs from refrigerator. In a pot, combine cream, vanilla extract, rosemary, caster sugar, lemon zest and olive oil and bring to a simmer. Do not boil or the cream will split. Remove from the heat, leave for 5 minutes, then remove the rosemary.

2 Whisk the single egg and the extra yolks in a separate bowl.

3 Return the cream mixture to the stove and bring to the scald again (do not boil). Add half of the cream mixture to the egg mixture while whisking to combine. Add the newly combined mixture to the remaining cream mixture in the saucepan and stir to combine and thicken slightly.

4 Remove the pan from the heat and place into a large bowl of iced water to cool rapidly.

5 Fill individual ramekins with mixture, place in a deep baking dish and place into the oven. Add enough water to the dish to come halfway up the sides of the ramekins. Cover with a sheet of greaseproof paper and cook until set: approximately 30–40 minutes.

6 Cool to room temperature and then refrigerate. When cool, top with caster sugar and burn with a cooking blowtorch or under a grill until caramelised.

NUTRITIONAL VALUE PER SERVE   FAT **115** G   CARBOHYDRATE **34** G   PROTEIN **8** G

Ricotta fritters with orange sauce

INGREDIENTS

sauce
1 cup orange juice, strained
$\frac{1}{3}$ cup caster sugar
2 tablespoons butter
2 tablespoons cream
1 tablespoon triple sec or cointreau
fritters
1 cup oil, for frying
250 g fresh ricotta, mashed
$\frac{1}{4}$ cup plain flour, sifted
$2\frac{1}{2}$ tablespoons caster sugar
2 eggs
1 tablespoon orange zest
2 tablespoons icing sugar
1 orange, segmented
serves 4

PREPARATION TIME
10 minutes

COOKING TIME
15 minutes

1 In a small saucepan, combine the orange juice, sugar, butter, cream and triple sec. Heat until butter has melted, and bring to the boil. Reduce the heat and simmer until the sauce thickens.

2 Heat the oil in a large frying pan. Place the ricotta, flour, caster sugar, eggs and orange zest in a large bowl and mix together until well combined.

3 Place 1 tablespoon of mixture in the hot oil to make each fritter. Cook 3–4 at a time for 1–2 minutes each, turning over to cook on both sides. Take out with a slotted spoon and drain on paper towel.

4 To serve the fritters, pour over the orange sauce, dust with icing sugar and garnish with orange segments.

NUTRITIONAL VALUE PER SERVE	FAT 51 G	CARBOHYDRATE 51 G	PROTEIN 12.5 G

Individual fig puddings

INGREDIENTS

250 g dried figs, chopped
1 cup water
1 teaspoon bicarbonate of soda
2 eggs
60 g butter
³/₄ cup caster sugar
1 cup self-raising flour
1 vanilla bean
1 teaspoon vanilla extract
butterscotch sauce
1 cup brown sugar
20 ml cream
30 g unsalted butter
serves 4

PREPARATION TIME
5 minutes

COOKING TIME
50 minutes

1 Preheat the oven to 190°C. Place the figs, water and bicarbonate of soda in a saucepan and cook for about 20 minutes, or until mixture has reached a jam consistency.

2 Pour the fig mixture into a bowl and beat in the remaining ingredients. Split the vanilla bean down the middle, scrape out the seeds and add them to the mixture.

3 Pour the mixture into individual ramekins or timbale-moulds and bake for 25 minutes.

4 To make the butterscotch sauce, combine all the ingredients in a saucepan, and stir over a low heat until sugar dissolves.

5 Serve the individual puddings with the sauce and cream or ice-cream.

NUTRITIONAL VALUE PER SERVE   FAT 16.5 G   CARBOHYDRATE 93 G   PROTEIN 6.5 G

Hazelnut brownies

INGREDIENTS

$^1/_2$ cup unsweetened chocolate pieces
1 cup plain flour
2 teaspoons cocoa
$^1/_2$ teaspoon baking powder
$^1/_2$ teaspoon salt
90 g butter
150 ml extra virgin olive oil
1 tablespoon vanilla extract
2 cups sugar
4 eggs
1$^1/_2$ cup hazelnuts, coarsely chopped
makes approximately 2 dozen

PREPARATION TIME
8 minutes, plus
30 minutes refrigeration

COOKING TIME
30 minutes

1 Preheat the oven to 180°C. Line a 20 cm square baking dish with greaseproof paper. Melt the chocolate slowly in 30-second intervals in the microwave on a medium heat.

2 Sift together the flour, cocoa, baking powder and salt into a separate bowl and set aside.

3 Melt the butter and beat with the olive oil, vanilla extract and sugar in a large bowl until combined. Add the eggs one at a time, then stir in the melted chocolate.

4 Gently stir in all dry ingredients, being careful not to over-mix. Add one cup of hazelnuts.

5 Pour the mixture into the greased and lined baking tin and sprinkle over the remaining hazelnuts. Bake for 25–30 minutes, until the brownies begin to pull away from the sides of the pan. Test with a skewer: they should still be soft but not raw-looking.

6 Cool in the baking tray on a wire rack and then refrigerate for 30 minutes before cutting into squares.

NUTRITIONAL VALUE PER SERVE	FAT 15 G	CARBOHYDRATE 23 G	PROTEIN 3 G

Glossary

Al dente: Italian term to describe pasta and rice that are cooked until tender but still firm to the bite.

Asafoetida: a herbaceous perennial plant native to Iran. The dried sap is used as a spice. It resembles onion and garlic in flavour.

Bake blind: to bake pastry cases without their fillings. Line the raw pastry case with greaseproof paper and fill with raw rice or dried beans to prevent collapsed sides and puffed base. Remove paper and fill 5 minutes before completion of cooking time.

Baste: to spoon hot cooking liquid over food at intervals during cooking to moisten and flavour it.

Beat: to make a mixture smooth with rapid and regular motions using a spatula, wire whisk or electric mixer; to make a mixture light and smooth by enclosing air.

Beurre manié: equal quantities of butter and flour mixed together to a smooth paste and stirred bit by bit into a soup, stew or sauce while on the heat to thicken. Stop adding when desired thickness results.

Bind: to add egg or a thick sauce to hold ingredients together when cooked.

Blanch: to plunge some foods into boiling water for less than a minute and immediately plunge into iced water. This is to brighten the colour of some vegetables; to remove skin from tomatoes and nuts.

Blend: to mix 2 or more ingredients thoroughly together; do not confuse with blending in an electric blender.

Boil: to cook in a liquid brought to boiling point and kept there.

Boiling point: when bubbles rise continually and break over the entire surface of the liquid, reaching a temperature of 100°C (212°F). In some cases food is held at this high temperature for a few seconds then heat is turned to low for slower cooking. See simmer.

Bouquet garni: a bundle of several herbs tied together with string for easy removal, placed into pots of stock, soups and stews for flavour. A few sprigs of fresh thyme, parsley and bay leaf are used. Can be purchased in sachet form for convenience.

Caramelise: to heat sugar in a heavy-based pan until it liquefies and develops a caramel colour. Vegetables such as blanched carrots and sautéed onions may be sprinkled with sugar and caramelised.

Chill: to place in the refrigerator or stir over ice until cold.

Clarify: to make a liquid clear by removing sediments and impurities. To melt fat and remove any sediment.

Coat: to dust or roll food items in flour to cover the surface before the food is cooked. Also, to coat in flour, egg and breadcrumbs.

Cool: to stand at room temperature until some or all heat is removed, e.g. cool a little, cool completely.

Cream: to make creamy and fluffy by working the mixture with the back of a wooden spoon, usually refers to creaming butter and sugar or margarine. May also be creamed with an electric mixer.

Croutons: small cubes of bread, toasted or fried, used as an addition to salads or as a garnish to soups and stews.

Crudite: raw vegetable sticks served with a dipping sauce.

Crumb: to coat foods in flour, egg and breadcrumbs to form a protective coating for foods which are fried. Also adds flavour, texture and enhances appearance.

Cube: to cut into small pieces with six even sides, e.g. cubes of meat.

Cut in: to combine fat and flour using 2 knives scissor fashion or with a pastry blender, to make pastry.

Deglaze: to dissolve dried out cooking juices left on the base and sides of a roasting dish or frying pan. Add a little water, wine or stock, scrape and stir over heat until dissolved. Resulting liquid is used to make a flavoursome gravy or added to a sauce or casserole.

Degrease: to skim fat from the surface of cooking liquids, e.g. stocks, soups, casseroles.

Dice: to cut into small cubes.

Dredge: to heavily coat with icing sugar, sugar, flour or cornflour.

Dressing: a mixture added to completed dishes to add moisture and flavour, e.g. salads, cooked vegetables.

Drizzle: to pour in a fine thread-like stream moving over a surface.

Egg wash: beaten egg with milk or water used to brush over pastry, bread dough or biscuits to give a sheen and golden brown colour.

Essence: a strong flavouring liquid, usually made by distillation. Only a few drops are needed to flavour.

Fillet: a piece of prime meat, fish or poultry which is boneless or has all bones removed.

Flake: to separate cooked fish into flakes, removing any bones and skin, using 2 forks.

Flame: to ignite warmed alcohol over food or to pour into a pan with food, ignite then serve.

Flute: to make decorative indentations around the pastry rim before baking.

Fold in: combining of a light, whisked or creamed mixture with other ingredients. Add a portion of the other ingredients at a time and mix using a gentle circular motion, over and under the mixture so that air will not be lost. Use a silver spoon or spatula.

Glaze: to brush or coat food with a liquid that will give the finished product a glossy appearance, and on baked products, a golden brown colour.

Grease: to rub the surface of a metal or heatproof dish with oil or fat, to prevent the food from sticking.

Herbed butter: softened butter mixed with finely chopped fresh herbs and re-chilled. Used to serve on grilled meats and fish.

Hors d'oeuvre: small savoury foods served as an appetiser, popularly known today as 'finger food'.

Infuse: to steep foods in a liquid until the liquid absorbs their flavour.

Joint: to cut poultry and game into serving pieces by dividing at the joint.

Julienne: to cut some food, e.g. vegetables and processed meats, into fine strips the length of matchsticks. Used for inclusion in salads or as a garnish to cooked dishes.

Knead: to work a yeast dough in a pressing, stretching and folding motion with the heel of the hand until smooth and elastic to develop the gluten strands. Non-yeast doughs should be lightly and quickly handled as gluten development is not desired.

Line: to cover the inside of a baking tin with paper for the easy removal of the cooked product from the baking tin.

Macerate: to stand fruit in a syrup, liqueur or spirit to give added flavour.

Marinade: a flavoured liquid, into which food is placed for some time to give it flavour and to tenderise. Marinades include an acid ingredient such as vinegar or wine, oil and seasonings.

Mask: to evenly cover cooked food portions with a sauce, mayonnaise or savoury jelly.

Pan-fry: to fry foods in a small amount of fat or oil, sufficient to coat the base of the pan.

Parboil: to boil until partially cooked. The food is then finished by some other method.

Pare: to peel the skin from vegetables and fruit. Peel is the popular term but pare is the name given to the knife used; paring knife.

Pit: to remove stones or seeds from olives, cherries, dates.

Pith: the white lining between the rind and flesh of oranges, grapefruit and lemons.

Pitted: the olives, cherries, dates etc. with the stone removed, e.g. purchase pitted dates.

Poach: to simmer gently in enough hot liquid to almost cover the food so shape will be retained.

Pound: to flatten meats with a meat mallet; to reduce to a paste or small particles with a mortar and pestle.

Simmer: to cook in liquid just below boiling point at about 96°C (205°F) with small bubbles rising gently to the surface.

Skim: to remove fat or froth from the surface of simmering food.

Stock: the liquid produced when meat, poultry, fish or vegetables have been simmered in water to extract the flavour. Used as a base for soups, sauces, casseroles etc. Convenience stock products are available.

Sweat: to cook sliced onions or vegetables, in a small amount of butter in a covered pan over low heat, to soften them and release flavour without colouring.

Conversions

Measurements differ from country to country, so it's important to understand what the differences are. This Measurements Guide gives you simple 'at-a-glance' information for using the recipes in this book, wherever you may be.

Cooking is not an exact science – minor variations in measurements won't make a difference to your cooking.

EQUIPMENT

There is a difference in the size of measuring cups used internationally, but the difference is minimal (only 2–3 teaspoons). We use the Australian standard metric measurements in our recipes:

1 teaspoon ....5 ml	1 tablespoon....20 ml
$^1/_2$ cup......125 ml	1 cup.....250 ml
4 cups...1 litre	

Measuring cups come in sets of one cup (250 ml), $^1/_2$ cup (125 ml), $^1/_3$ cup (80 ml) and $^1/_4$ cup (60 ml). Use these for measuring liquids and certain dry ingredients.

Measuring spoons come in a set of four and should be used for measuring dry and liquid ingredients.

When using cup or spoon measures always make them level (unless the recipe indicates otherwise).

DRY VERSUS WET INGREDIENTS

While this system of measures is consistent for liquids, it's more difficult to quantify dry ingredients. For instance, one level cup equals: 200 g of brown sugar; 210 g of caster sugar; and 110 g of icing sugar.

When measuring dry ingredients such as flour, don't push the flour down or shake it into the cup. It is best just to spoon the flour in until it reaches the desired amount. When measuring liquids use a clear vessel indicating metric levels.

Always use medium eggs (55–60 g) when eggs are required in a recipe.

OVEN

Your oven should always be at the right temperature before placing the food in it to be cooked. Note that if your oven doesn't have a fan you may need to cook food for a little longer.

MICROWAVE

It is difficult to give an exact cooking time for microwave cooking. It is best to watch what you are cooking closely to monitor its progress.

STANDING TIME

Many foods continue to cook when you take them out of the oven or microwave. If a recipe states that the food needs to 'stand' after cooking, be sure not to overcook the dish.

CAN SIZES

The can sizes available in your supermarket or grocery store may not be the same as specified in the recipe. Don't worry if there is a small variation in size – it's unlikely to make a difference to the end result.

dry		liquids	
metric (grams)	imperial (ounces)	metric (millilitres)	imperial (fluid ounces)
		30 ml	1 fl oz
30 g	1 oz	60 ml	2 fl oz
60 g	2 oz	90 ml	3 fl oz
90 g	3 oz	100 ml	3 1/2 fl oz
100 g	3 1/2 oz	125 ml	4 fl oz
125 g	4 oz	150 ml	5 fl oz
150 g	5 oz	190 ml	6 fl oz
185 g	6 oz	250 ml	8 fl oz
200 g	7 oz	300 ml	10 fl oz
250 g	8 oz	500 ml	16 fl oz
280 g	9 oz	600 ml	20 fl oz (1 pint)*
315 g	10 oz	1000 ml (1 litre)	32 fl oz
330 g	11 oz		
370 g	12 oz		
400 g	13 oz		
440 g	14 oz		
470 g	15 oz		
500 g	16 oz (1 lb)		
750 g	24 oz (1 1/2 lb)		
1000 g (1 kg)	32 oz (2 lb)	*Note: an American pint is 16 fl oz.	

cooking temperatures	°C (celsius)	°F (fahrenheit)	gas mark
very slow	120	250	1/2
slow	150	300	2
moderately slow	160	315	2–3
moderate	180	350	4
moderate hot	190	375	5
	200	400	6
hot	220	425	7
very hot	230	450	8
	240	475	9
	250	500	10

Index